AN INSTANT GUIDE TO

SEABIRDS

The most common seabirds of North
American coasts
described and illustrated in full color

Mike Lambert and Alan Pearson

BONANZA BOOKS
New York

© 1988 Atlantis Publications Ltd

All rights reserved. No part of this publication
may be reproduced, stored in a retrieval system,
or transmitted, in any form or by any means,
electronic, mechanical, photocopying, recording
or otherwise without the permission of
Crown Publishers, Inc. and the copyright holders.

First published 1988 by Bonanza Books,
distributed by Crown Publishers, Inc.

Printed in Spain

ISBN 0–517–65524–1

h g f e d c b a

Contents

Introduction

Out walking along the beach, on vacation by the coast or even out in a boat fishing in the ocean, you will see many of the birds that live in and around the sea. Of course, everyone knows — or thinks they know — what a gull looks like; but do you know the difference between, say, a Black-legged Kittiwake and a Laughing Gull? How do you tell if the bird you are watching is indeed a Gull and not a Tern?

This book, like the earlier *Instant Guide to Birds*, will enable the reader and newcomer to birdwatching to identify positively and as simply as possible the great majority of birds found in and around the North American coastline. It provides a more detailed look at a broader selection of the species of birds you are likely to see around beaches, cliffs, estuaries and shorelines.

How to use this book

We have divided the book into nine sections, each indicated by a different color band at the top of the page (see Contents list on page 3). These sections are: **Grebes and Loons; Tube-noses; Large Seabirds; Ducks; Shorebirds; Skuas and Jaegers; Gulls, Terns and Skimmer; Auks; Saltwater-related Species.**

Within each of these color-coded sections the birds are featured in ascending size order, the measurements given being from the point of the bill to the tip of the tail. Each size range is represented by a symbol (see Fig. 1) which is featured in the color band at the top of each page. To identify your bird, estimate its size and then decide to which section it belongs, using the *Guide to Identification* which follows.

Fig. 1 Guide to bird sizes

 Small
6½–9¾in

 Medium
10–15in

 Large
15½–27in

 Very large
28–62in

Additional information in this color band tells you whether the bird is a resident, a winter or summer visitor, or an internal migrant.

Guide to Identification

Page numbers given at the end of each section will enable you to turn directly to the relevant section of the book.

Grebes and Loons are fully aquatic birds. Their legs are placed towards the tail to provide strong propulsion for swimming and diving. They rarely visit land where they are ungainly and vulnerable. Their strongest characteristic is that they appear virtually tailless in flight, with large webbed feet trailing behind and a marked "drooped" head and neck. **14–18**

Tube-noses include the Shearwaters, Storm-Petrels and the Northern Fulmar. They are wanderers of the oceans and the larger birds fly on stiff straight wings. Storm-Petrels flutter and weave just above the water. The term "tube-nose" refers to the external nostrils on the upper mandible of these birds. **19–33**

Large Seabirds include species larger than all except the very largest gulls. Their long wings and heavy bodies should prevent confusion with birds of any other section. **34–44**

Ducks are characterized by heavy bodies, flattened bills and pointed tails. Sea-ducks are normally stockier than their inland counterparts, usually keeping in small flocks. Only the Merganser has a long slim bill. **45–56**

Shorebirds are a large and numerous group of birds found on and around water margins. Most have long legs for wading in shallow water and fairly long bills. They are rapid feeders, often in large flocks and this section contains many species with similar markings, often only seen at a distance across mud flats or estuaries. Careful observation is necessary to avoid confusion and make a positive identification. **57–80**

Skuas and Jaegers are large dark seabirds. They actually look aggressive with their powerful builds and strong direct flight. They are notorious for robbing other birds of fish, forcing them to disgorge their catch by continuous harassment. Central tail feathers often aid identification. **81–85**

Gulls, Terns and Skimmer are very familiar coastal birds. Graceful and skilled in flight, their plumages almost invariably consist of combinations of gray, black and white, although bills and feet do vary. Plunge-divers and/or scavengers, these species are very visible when feeding. The Skimmer is unique in its feeding method, slicing the water surface with its lower mandible to trap fish near the surface. **86–104**

Auks are a very distinctive group of "penguin-like" birds which fly low over the water with a whirring wing action. They are skilled at swimming underwater to catch their prey. They breed in huge colonies. **105–117**

Saltwater-related Species include a selection of birds which, although less obviously associated with water than the individually featured species, are nevertheless dependent on a saltwater environment. They are grouped according to habitat.   118–121

Making a positive identification

Once you have decided on the section to which your bird belongs, you can turn to the pages on which the individual species are described and illustrated. Your estimate of size will be helpful at this point to locate the bird within its section.

In the first box of text on each page, you will find described the feature or combination of features that are unique to that bird in that size range. It may be that only one piece of information is necessary as with the "remarkable scuttling run" of the Sanderling, or the "dark gray wings tipped with solid black" of the Laughing Gull. If you are certain of these features, which are also shown on the color illustration of each bird, then you have already made a positive identification and need read on only out of interest and to build up a more detailed picture of the bird.

If you are uncertain about these specific features, the second box completes the description and adds details for sexes and juveniles.

The third box deals with characteristic habits, range and habitat. The information on habitat and range can be used in conjunction with the distribution map featured for each bird.

Fig. 2 Distribution Map

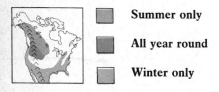

Summer only

All year round

Winter only

Although the second and third boxes provide additional useful information, they do not specifically identify the particular bird. Only the first box can do that.

Lookalikes

The fourth box on each page gives the names of similar birds with which the featured bird could be confused. All these **Lookalikes** are either featured in detail themselves or appear in the final section of the book (Saltwater-related species) grouped by habitat.

This Lookalikes box is important for two reasons. Firstly, it is very easy to jump to conclusions when looking for known identifying features. So check the Lookalikes carefully. Size is easily misjudged and buff plumage, for instance, often mistaken for yellow. This box will give you other possibilities to consider.

Secondly it is very important for the observer to be aware of exactly what points he should be looking for, as a means of quickly distinguishing similar birds. This is where guesswork ends and skill begins.

Now you are ready to use this book. It is designed to fit into your pocket, so take it with you on your next trip. Good birdwatching, and don't forget to check your sightings on the check-list provided with the index!

Fig. 3 Specimen page

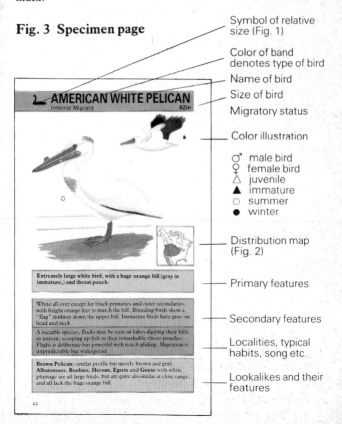

Symbol of relative size (Fig. 1)

Color of band denotes type of bird

Name of bird

Size of bird

Migratory status

Color illustration

♂ male bird
♀ female bird
△ juvenile
▲ immature
○ summer
● winter

Distribution map (Fig. 2)

Primary features

Secondary features

Localities, typical habits, song etc.

Lookalikes and their features

Glossary of terms

Adult A mature bird capable of breeding.

Bar A relatively narrow band of color across the area described, e.g. wing bars on a Surfbird.

Bib A distinctively colored patch between throat and breast e.g. Ancient Murrelet.

Call A few notes, or even a single note, indicating alarm or acting as a simple statement of presence.

Crest Erectile feathers on the crown, usually prominent during display, e.g. Pelagic Cormorant.

Display A ritualized pattern of behavior, usually movement, by which birds communicate, particularly during courtship and in defense of territory.

Immature A fully grown bird not yet old enough to breed, often in plumage markedly different from the adult.

Internal migrant Species present throughout the year within North America, but with the population showing consistent migration according to the seasons, e.g. Bufflehead.

Juvenile A young bird in its own first plumage variation, having left the nest but not completed its first molt at the end of summer.

Mandible The bill is composed of the upper and lower mandibles.

Migratory Any species exhibiting movement consistent with the change of seasons is a migratory species.

Molt Change of plumage, usually before winter and before breeding.

Passage migrant A migratory species, usually seen briefly in spring and/or fall, en route to its breeding or wintering grounds, e.g. White-rumped Sandpiper.

Patch An area of color, perhaps on the neck, e.g. Common Loon.

Pelagic Normally to be found out at sea, only visiting land to breed.

Phase Color variations within a distinct species, often associated with a change of range.

Range That area which contains the vast proportion of the population of the species considered.

Resident Present throughout the year, e.g. Masked Booby; the local population may be supplemented by partial migrants from adjoining areas.

Shield A structure, lacking feathers, on the forehead of some water birds, e.g. King Eider.

Species A group of individuals (population) whose members resemble each other more closely than they resemble members of other populations and which, almost invariably, are capable of breeding only amongst themselves.

Speculum A panel on the trailing edge of the inner wing feathers of ducks, usually highly and distinctively colored, see Fig. 4.

Stripe A relatively narrow, long band of color along the area described, e.g. the stripe along the bill of a Thick-billed Murre.

Subspecies A group of individuals within a species which differ slightly, usually in plumage, from the typical form but which are capable of breeding with any individual of that species.

Summer visitor A migratory species, arriving in spring and returning to its winter home at the end of the breeding season, e.g. Magnificent Frigatebird.

Winter visitor A migratory species, arriving in late fall and returning to its summer home to breed when conditions there improve in spring, e.g. Thayer's Gull.

Fig. 4 The parts of a bird

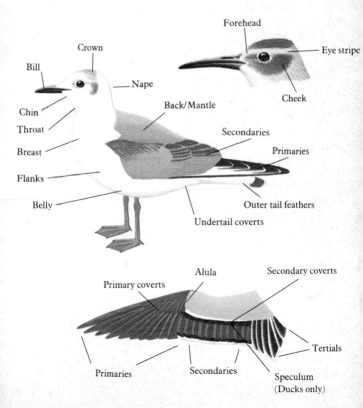

13

Apparently tailless, Grebes look short-bodied. Flight is labored with drooped neck extended.

Eared Grebe (1) 13in Res/Int. Mig. Summer: colorful fanned ear tufts, black neck. Winter: dark ear coverts remain. Uptilted bill. Nests on freshwater lakes.

Horned Grebe (2) 13½in Int. Mig. Summer: colorful ear tufts, chestnut neck. Winter: white cheeks & ear coverts. Straight bill. Nests on freshwater lakes & ponds.

Pied-billed Grebe (3) 13½in Res/ Summer Vis. Summer: black ring round bill. Winter: deep, pale bill unmarked. Secretive. Nests on marshes, ponds.

Red-necked Grebe (4) 18in Int. Mig. Summer: red neck, pale gray cheeks. Winter: white crescent above dusky neck. Slim black & yellow "dagger" bill. Nests on freshwater lakes.

Western Grebe (5) 25in Int. Mig. Summer & winter: long swan-like black & white neck. Slim, uptilted yellow bill. Large size. Nests on freshwater lakes.

Slender, uptilted bill, and dark red throat patch in summer.

Dark back, striped nape, plain gray head and side of neck, white below. Winter and immature birds have white-spotted backs, and appear somewhat paler above than other Loons.

Note Loons' flight profile, with neck and head slung low. Also noted for swimming low. Nest in tundra lakes. Migrate to coasts in winter, seen inland on passage (and casually.) Only Loon to rise from water without "running."

Common Loon: bill is heavy, dagger-like. Glossy dark green head in summer. **Yellow-billed Loon:** heavy uptilted ivory yellow bill. **Arctic Loon:** slender dagger-like bill. Back checkered in summer. **Mergansers:** slim red bills. **Ducks:** flattened bills. **Cormorants:** hooked bills.

15

Fairly slender dagger-like bill, and dark purple throat patch in summer.

Heavily checkered back and striped neck, with plain gray head and nape. White below, other colors fade to gray in winter and in immatures, with a distinct white/gray demarcation through the eye.

Loons have striking flight profiles, the neck and head being slung low. They are also noted for swimming low. Nest in tundra lakes. Migrate to west coast in winter, being seen inland on passage.

Common Loon: heavy dagger-like bill. Glossy dark green head in summer. **Yellow-billed Loon:** heavy uptilted ivory yellow bill. **Red-throated Loon:** slender uptilted bill. Back not checkered in summer. **Mergansers:** slim red bills. **Ducks:** flattened bills. **Cormorants:** hooked bills.

Heavy black dagger-like bill, and glossy dark green head in summer.

Mostly pied plumage, a heavily checkered back, striped patch on neck, stripes into spots on flanks. White below, but other colors fade to gray in winter adult and resemble immatures.

Loons have striking flight profiles, the neck and head being slung low. They are also noted for swimming low. Common Loons nest in wooded lakes giving remarkable yodeling call. Winter on the coast.

Yellow-billed Loon: yellow bill. **Arctic** and **Red-throated Loons:** dark gray bills are quite slender. Gray-headed in summer. **Mergansers:** smaller, slim red bills. **Ducks:** smaller, flattened bills. **Cormorants:** hooked bills.

17

Heavy, uptilted ivory yellow bill. Glossy dark green head in summer.

Mostly pied plumage, heavily checkered back, striped patch on neck, stripes into spots on flanks. White below, other colors fade to gray in winter adults to resemble immatures. These plumages are paler-headed than Common Loons.

Loons have striking flight profiles, the neck and head being slung low. They are also noted for swimming low. Nest in tundra lakes. Winter on west coast only, mainly in Canada.

Common Loon: heavy black dagger-like bill. **Arctic** and **Red-throated Loons:** quite slender dark gray bills. Gray-headed in summer. **Mergansers:** smaller, slim red bills. **Ducks:** smaller, flattened bills. **Cormorants:** hooked bills.

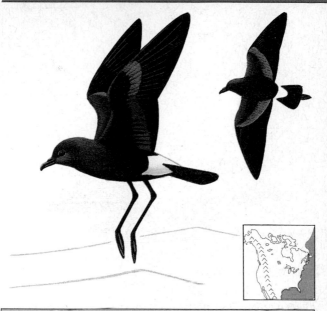

Small brownish black seabird with a white rump, and a square tail tip with feet projecting behind.

Delicate black tube-nosed bill, black legs and yellow webbed feet, a faint diagonal wing bar, are only visible at close range. Rather short, rounded wings, and white around tail are discernible. All ages, sexes, alike.

Thoroughly pelagic, often seen following ships with a quick fluttering flight. Frequently hovers and "walks" on water with pattering feet. An Antarctic breeder, it visits the east coast in summer. Range is truly worldwide.

Leach's Storm-Petrel: white (faintly divided) rump with a longish clearly forked tail. Other **Storm-Petrels** are all black or pale gray, and all lack white rump. **Black Tern:** inland or coastal. Gray rump and tail, pale underwings.

19

Small brownish black seabird with a white (but faintly divided) rump, and a longish forked tail. (Californian birds may be brown-rumped.)

Delicate black tube-nosed bill. Black legs, and feet which do not project beyond tail, the faint wing bar, are only visible at close range. Long pointed wings, black undertail, are easier features to identify. All ages, sexes, are alike.

Thoroughly pelagic, rarely seen following ships. Has an erratic bounding flight with tern-like beats and glides. It even hangs on the breeze, feet pattering. Breeds on northeastern and western coasts, migrating to Tropics in winter.

Wilson's Storm-Petrel: white rump. Square tail tip with feet projecting behind. Other **Storm-Petrels:** all black or pale gray, and all lack white rump. **Black Tern:** inland or coastal. Gray rump, tail. (Note **Black Storm-Petrel** differs from Californian birds by deep, lazy wing beats.)

Small all dark seabird with shallow wing beats and a fluttering, but direct, flight.

The delicate tube-nosed bill, legs, feet, are black. Plumage overall is brown-black, with a noticeable paler bar on both under- and upperwing. The legs do not project beyond the tail, which is forked. All ages and sexes are alike.

Thoroughly pelagic, but rarely seen following ships, it is a resident species, breeding off the coast of California with only a slightly extended winter range down to Mexico.

Black Storm-Petrel: all dark, but flies with deliberate and deep wing action. (Note **Leach's Storm-Petrel:** brown-rumped Californian form has erratic bounding flight.) Other **Storm-Petrels** have white rumps, or are pale gray. **Black Tern:** inland or coastal. Gray rump, tail. Pale underwings.

Small, tube-nosed seabird, blue-gray above, paler below.

Bill, legs and feet are black. Dark smudge round eye. Forehead, primaries and wing coverts particularly dark, but overall appearance at sea is of a very pale bird. The long tail is forked. All ages and sexes are alike.

A resident of the north Pacific, it breeds widely on islands along western coastline, particularly Alaska. Frequently seen following ships, it has a shallow flight interspersed with glides.

Other **Storm-Petrels** are all dark or dark with white rumps. **Black Tern:** inland or coastal. Straight slim bill. **Red** and **Red-necked Phalaropes** (winter): only confused at a distance in flight. Longish bills and white rump divided by black will confirm.

Small all dark seabird with deep, lazy wing beats giving a deliberate, buoyant flight.

The delicate tube-nosed bill, legs and feet, are black. The plumage overall is brown-black, although there is a noticeable paler bar on the upperwing. The wings are long. The tail is long and forked. All ages and sexes are alike.

Thoroughly pelagic, sometimes following ships, it is a summer visitor to southwestern coasts, breeding on islands off California. It migrates only as far as northwest South America, spending a long season on our coasts.

Ashy Storm-Petrel: all dark, but flies with a fluttering and less deep wing action. (Note **Leach's Storm-Petrel:** brown-rumped Californian form has erratic bounding flight.) Other **Storm-Petrels** have white rumps, or are pale gray. **Black Tern:** inland or coastal. Gray rump, tail.

A small brown and white shearwater, tube-nosed, with a brown
undertail and fluttering flight.

Slim black bill. Brown upperparts. Longish wings are white
below with quite wide brown margins and wing tips. The tail is
fairly long and the legs are mainly pink. All ages and sexes are
alike.

A pelagic species breeding in the Tropics worldwide, birds arrive
on the east coast in greatest numbers in late summer, some birds
stay in the Caribbean all year round. Swim after food, do not
usually follow boats.

Manx Shearwater: black and white, rapid tilting flight, white
undertail. **Buller's Shearwater:** west coast only. Other
Shearwaters, "light phase" **Northern Fulmar:** significantly
larger and/or lack sharp color demarcation. **Auks** have "frantic"
wing-action, stout shape.

A small black and white shearwater, tube-nosed, with white undertail and rapid tilting flight.

Slim black bill, black above. Long, slim wings are white below with black margins, darker wing tips. Legs are mainly pink. All ages and sexes are alike.

A numerous pelagic species breeding across the north Atlantic. They migrate to South American coasts in late summer and fall, passing east coast. Flight is stiff-winged, "shearing" the wave-tops at speed. Do not follow boats.

Audubon's Shearwater: brown and white, fluttering flight, brown undertail. **Buller's Shearwater:** west coast only. Other **Shearwaters**, "light phase" **Northern Fulmar:** significantly larger and/or lack sharp color demarcation. **Auks** have "frantic" wing-action, stout shape.

Winter visitor to west coast, wholly brown-black with dull gray underwing coverts. Dark gray bill, legs. Strong direct flight.

Slim tube-nosed bill. Upperwings plain, with underwing primaries and secondaries the same color. Underparts slightly paler than upperparts. All ages and sexes are alike.

A pelagic species breeding around Australia in our winter, seen off Alaska in summer and on return migration down the west coast. Not common, but gregarious when seen. Plunge-dive for food, sometimes following boats.

Sooty Shearwater: summer visitor to both coastlines, silvery underwing coverts. **Flesh-footed Shearwater:** summer visitor, triangles on wings, pink legs, bill, and unhurried flight. "Dark phase" **Northern Fulmar:** blunt yellow bill. Other similar seabirds have white underparts.

Summer visitor to east and west coasts, wholly brown-black with silvery underwing coverts. Dark gray bill, legs. Strong direct flight.

Slim tube-nosed bill. Upperwings plain, with the silvery markings on the underwing appearing as a distinct flash, even at distance. Underparts slightly paler than upperparts. All ages and sexes are alike.

A pelagic species breeding around New Zealand and Chile in our winter, they arrive on coast in summer sometimes in flocks of a hundred thousand or more. Plunge-dive for food.

Short-tailed Shearwater: winter visitor to west coast only, dull gray underwing coverts. **Flesh-footed Shearwater:** west coast only, triangles on wings, pink legs and bill, unhurried flight. "Dark phase" **Northern Fulmar:** blunt yellow bill. Other similar seabirds have white underparts.

Sharply defined color demarcation, with M pattern picked out on upperwing by "frosted" gray plumage.

Blue-black tube-nosed bill. Brown-black upperparts with gray mantle, rump, and secondaries. Underparts brilliant white with a thin dark margin around underwing. Tail wedge-shaped, feet pinkish. All ages, sexes, alike.

A pelagic species breeding off New Zealand in our winter, they arrive on northwestern coasts in summer, migrating southwards on the return journey. Their slim build provides a graceful flight, skimming low for food. Gregarious.

Pink-footed Shearwater: pink-billed. Indistinct demarcation between dark and white colors. Other white-bodied **Shearwaters** are all seen on the east coast. "Light phase" **Northern Fulmar:** blunt yellow bill, white head. **Gulls:** lack tube nose.

Summer visitor to west coast, wholly brown-black showing triangles on wings. Pink bill, legs. Unhurried flight.

Slim tube-nosed bill, black tip. Upperwing tips have black triangles, underwing tips silvery triangles. Good light may be needed to spot these markings. All ages and sexes are alike.

A pelagic species breeding off New Zealand in our winter, they arrive off North America in summer. They both dive and skim the water for food, sometimes "treading" the surface. Gregarious.

Sooty Shearwater: silvery underwing coverts, dark gray bill and legs, strong, direct flight (possibly east coast.) **Short-tailed Shearwater:** winter visitor, dull gray underwing coverts, dark gray bill, legs. Strong direct flight. "Dark phase" **Northern Fulmar:** blunt yellow bill.

Blunt yellow tube-nosed bill. Flies wheeling on rigid wings with noticeable pale patches in primaries.

Gray back, upperwing, tail. "Dark phase" Pacific birds gray overall. "Light phase" Atlantic birds have white head, underwing and underparts. Intermediates may be seen but look for bullneck and buff legs.

This ocean-going species breeds on cliff ledges in loose colonies. Magnificent fliers, they drift on air currents quite unlike gulls, giving a few stiff wingbeats, then long glides. Seen mostly in winter following boats.

Gulls: lack tube nose and bullneck, and fly with more deliberate wing beats. **Shearwaters** have slimmer tube-nosed bills, their build is lighter, and their tilting flight is at wave level.

Pink-billed, pink-footed west coast shearwater with indistinct demarcation between dark and white colors.

Bill tip dark. Upperparts dark brown. Chin and throat whitish, underparts white mottled with brown, especially undertail, flanks. Underwing also mottled, with wide ill-defined dark margins, wing tips. All ages, sexes, alike.

A pelagic species breeding off Chile, it migrates north arriving during summer months on the west coast. Flight is slow and deliberate, alternating with long glides. May be gregarious or solitary.

Buller's Shearwater: sharply defined color demarcation, with M pattern on upperwing. "Light phase" **Northern Fulmar:** blunt yellow bill, white head. Other white-bodied **Shearwaters** are all seen on the east coast. **Gulls:** lack tube nose.

31

Long, heavy, yellowish tube-nosed bill, with a faint band.
Indistinct demarcation between dark and white colors.
Indistinct "horseshoe" on rump.

Uniform gray-brown upperparts shade to white underparts.
Underwings are white with a brown margin and wing tips. Legs
are pink. All ages and sexes are alike.

A pelagic species breeding on mid-Atlantic and Mediterranean
islands, arriving off the east coast in late summer and fall. They
have a lazy, unhurried flight, and skim or dive for food, often
following fishing boats.

Greater Shearwater: brown-capped over white face, clear white
"horseshoe" on rump. **Pink-footed** and **Buller's Shearwaters:**
west coast. **Manx** and **Audubon's Shearwaters:** much smaller.
"Light phase" **Northern Fulmar:** white head, blunt bill. **Jaegers,
Gulls:** lack tube nose.

Brown cap over white cheeks and nape. White "horseshoe" on rump.

Heavy, black tube-nosed bill. Dark brown back, upperwings, uppertail, undertail. Legs pink. Underparts are mostly white, with some brown across belly, and around underwings. All ages and sexes are alike.

A pelagic species breeding on south Atlantic islands in spring, they arrive on east coast in summer. Flying with quick, strong beats on rigid wings, diving from some height for food, they often follow fishing boats.

Cory's Shearwater: yellow-billed. Indistinct "horseshoe" on rump, and demarcation about head. **Pink-footed, Buller's Shearwaters:** west coast only. **Manx, Audubon's Shearwaters:** much smaller, black bills. "Light phase" **Northern Fulmar:** white head, blunt bill. **Jaegers, Gulls:** lack tube nose.

33

Medium-large dark seabird, adults with red facial skin (difficult to see) and white flank patches. Juveniles distinguished from other cormorants by smaller size.

Dark gray hooked bill. Irridescent greenish black body plumage with two prominent crests. The neck has a violet gloss with white plumes on breeding birds. Juveniles are dark brown overall, paler beneath.

A west coast cormorant, its small size is noticeable by the lower profile in the water, and the apparent loss of head in the straight flight profile. Gregarious, breeds on cliffs, both a coastal and deep water species.

Brandt's Cormorant: larger, adults have a blue throat pouch edged with buff feathers. **Great** and **Double-crested Cormorants:** obvious pale facial skin and pouch areas. **Loons:** heavy, dagger-like bills. No facial skin.

W

▲

Stout-billed, wedge-tailed seabird, with entirely chocolate brown upperparts. (Western birds have pale heads.)

Yellow bills (eastern birds gray) and feet. White underparts and inner underwings contrast sharply with the remaining dark brown. Juveniles and immatures are very similar except that white areas are speckled with brown.

Breeding around the Tropics, east and west of southern coasts, it is mostly seen at sea following ships or plunge-diving for fish. Often in groups, the flight action is fast, usually at low level. Will roost inshore.

Masked Booby: all ages show a dark trailing edge to both upper- and underwings. **Northern Gannet:** "golden"-headed at all ages except for white-speckled juveniles. **Pelicans** have huge bills and throat pouches.

35

Huge wingspan (7 feet,) dark body, western range.

Large hooked bill. Very dark overall in all ages with black feet.
Some white may be seen around the base of the bill, and on the
upper- and undertail of immatures and adults.

Thoroughly pelagic, it is usually seen following ships for fish or
garbage. Common at sea, especially in summer. It breeds on
islands of the central and western Pacific.

Magnificent Frigatebird: huge wingspan (over 7 feet.) Forked
tail which is sometimes folded. Eastern range. Dark bodied
Fulmars and **Shearwaters:** small by comparison with only half
the wingspan.

Large dark seabird, with a large area of orange facial skin and throat pouch.

Dark hooked bill. Plumage is very dark green overall. The crests vary, being whitish in the west, dark in the east. Immature birds are brown above, paler below.

Widespread, often seen in numbers in flight with characteristic head-up, bent-necked attitude. They swim low in the water and emerge to dry out with spread wings. Common coastally and inland around any major body of water.

Great Cormorant: small area of yellow facial skin and pouch, edged with white feathers. **Brandt's** and **Pelagic Cormorants:** facial skin dark colored. **Loons:** heavy dagger-like bills. No facial skin.

Stout-billed, wedge-tailed seabird, adult is white-headed, and all ages show a dark trailing edge to both upper- and underwings.

Black facial skin, yellowish bills and feet. Adults are white, with the tail and rear wing margins black. Juveniles and immatures have brown heads, and backs, with a white collar in between.

Breeding around the Tropics, east and west of southern coasts, it is normally seen over deep water performing high, vertical dives for fish, wings folded at entry. Fairly uncommon, it is usually seen in the Gulf of Mexico.

Northern Gannet: "golden"-headed at all ages except white-speckled juveniles. **Brown Booby:** continuous chocolate brown upperparts (western birds have pale heads.) **Pelicans** have huge bills and throat pouches.

Large dark seabird, with blue throat pouch edged with buff feathering.

Dark gray hooked bill. All of plumage is black with a dark oily gloss. Whitish plumes on head, neck, back and rump of breeding adults are absent on immatures. Juveniles are generally duller and browner.

Commonest west coast cormorant, it is exclusively pelagic, favoring rocky locations. In flight it has a distinctive straight head-and-neck posture, unlike other bent-necked cormorants. Appears very upright when at rest.

Pelagic Cormorant: smaller. Adults have red facial skin and white flank patches. **Great** and **Double-crested Cormorants:** obvious pale facial skin and pouch areas. **Loons:** heavy, dagger-like bills. No facial skin.

Large dark seabird, with white feathering around the small area of yellow facial skin and pouch.

Gray-yellow hooked bill. The dark body plumage is brown on the back, glossy black on the head, neck, and underparts. There is a bold white thigh patch. Immatures and juveniles are not so dark, with pale underparts and no thigh patch.

Widespread around the world, but only seen on eastern coasts, mainly in winter. Fly with a characteristic head-up, bent-necked attitude. They swim low in the water and emerge to dry out with spread wings.

Double-crested Cormorant: large area of orange facial skin and throat pouch. **Brandt's** and **Pelagic Cormorants:** facial skin dark-colored, not edged with white feathers. **Loons:** heavy dagger-like bills. No facial skin.

Stout-billed, wedge-tailed seabird, "golden"-headed at all ages except for the white-speckled juveniles.

Adults are all white except for black wing tips and feet, and the golden head. Juveniles are brown with speckles. Immatures show fewer dark areas over the three years to adulthood, with a spangled appearance.

The largest Atlantic seabird, breeding on northeastern coasts in huge colonies. Commonly seen further south in winter. Steady direct flight, often single file, contrasts with spectacular feeding dives, wings folded at entry.

Masked Booby: dark trailing edge to wings, with adults white-headed. Juveniles and immatures are brown-headed. **Brown Booby:** plain, chocolate brown upperparts. **Pelicans:** huge bills and throat pouches.

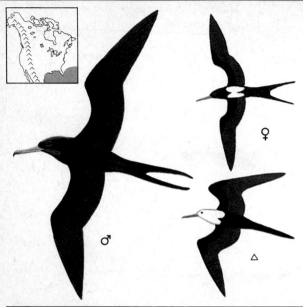

♀

♂

△

Huge wingspan (over 7 feet.) Forked tail which is sometimes folded. Eastern range.

Long hooked bill. Mostly brown-black with long, thin, angled wings and very long tail. Males have a red inflatable throat pouch. Females have white on underparts. Juveniles and immatures show varying amounts of white until adult.

Thoroughly pelagic, these excellent fliers can neither walk nor swim. Usually they glide or skim the water for food, but can dive spectacularly after fish or to harass other birds to disgorge fish. There is a breeding colony off Florida.

Black-footed Albatross: huge wingspan (7 feet,) dark body, western range.

Extremely large gray-brown bird, with a huge bill and throat pouch.

Adults are dark-bellied and pale-headed (white or yellow according to breeding condition,) breeding adults showing a chocolate brown hindneck. Juveniles are mostly brown.

A saltwater pelican, unusual in itself, this species is also noted for spectacular plunge-dives for fish, the wings being folded just before entry. It migrates erratically up and down both east and west coastlines.

Boobies and **Cormorants** with brown plumage are smaller, slimmer and have conventional bills in proportion to their size. **American White Pelican:** extremely large white bird, with a huge orange bill (gray in immature.)

Extremely large white bird, with a huge orange bill (gray in immature,) and throat pouch.

White all over except for black primaries and outer secondaries, with bright orange feet to match the bill. Breeding birds show a "flag" midway down the upper bill. Immature birds have gray on head and neck.

A sociable species, flocks may be seen on lakes dipping their bills in unison, scooping up fish in their remarkable throat pouches. Flight is deliberate but powerful with much gliding. Migration is unpredictable but widespread.

Brown Pelican: similar profile but mostly brown and gray.
Albatrosses, **Boobies**, **Herons**, **Egrets** and **Geese** with white plumage are all large birds, but are quite dissimilar at close range, and all lack the huge orange bill.

Small, puffy-headed duck, male with a large white triangle over the back of the head, female with a white cheek patch.

White wing patches visible in flight on dark wings and back. Male has a white body, breast, neck. The remainder of the head is black. Female has a brown head with gray back and dusky flanks.

Buffleheads migrate from nesting grounds on wooded lakes and ponds in Canada and the north, down to inland and coastal waters in the winter. This species is widespread and reasonably common.

Goldeneyes: larger with males showing white head patch before the eye. **Oldsquaw:** larger, plain dark wings.

Small, stub-billed duck, very dark overall, with no speculum visible.

Stocky build with steep forehead. Male has scattered white areas on otherwise slate-blue plumage, with dark red flanks. Female is brown with white "ear patch" and face markings. Pale belly.

A sea duck, this species nests alongside mountain streams, where it can be seen regularly on migration to its coastal wintering grounds. Here it favors rocky locations in heavy surf. Not gregarious, and does not mix with other species.

Scoters: larger and much bulkier. Bills are heavier and larger. Female **Bufflehead:** very small, white on innerwing. **Coot:** whitish bill and small red forehead shield.

Broad white stripe all along trailing upperwings, diminishing in primaries, especially on Lesser Scaup. Lesser (1;) Greater (2.)

Males have dark heads and necks (Lesser: purple, Greater: green,) black breasts, pale flanks (white on Greater) and gray backs. Females are brown overall with white at the base of the bill. All have gray bills, tipped black.

Highly migratory. The scarcer Greater Scaup breeds on the tundra, the Lesser Scaup across the northwest, both close to water. In winter both species form flocks, frequently mixed, in bays and estuaries. Diving ducks.

Canvasback males have chestnut heads, females lack white at base of bill. **Eiders, Scoters, Buffleheads, Goldeneyes** and **Mergansers:** white in the wing, either shown in the speculum only, and/or on the forewing. They are not alike when seen at rest.

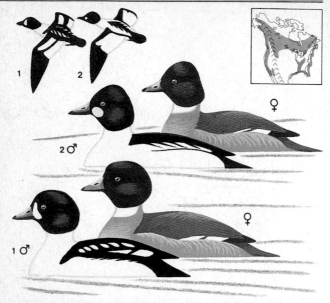

1
2
2♂
♀
1♂
♀

Dark-headed, white-necked ducks. Males have prominent white face marks between the bill and eye. Barrows (1;) Common (2.)

Prominent white wing patches show in flight. Barrow's male is purple-headed, Common is green-headed. Females' heads are brown. Males have black backs, white underparts. Females have dark backs and flanks, white bellies.

Sea ducks, they summer on lakes, nesting in nearby trees. Winter is spent on coasts or inland water. Excellent divers, observers may lose track of these birds as they travel great distances under water.

Bufflehead: smaller, white face patch behind eye. **Red-breasted Merganser:** long slim bill, no face patches.

Very dark duck overall, males showing an orange knob on the bill, females pale about the cheeks and throat.

Males are otherwise all black, females all dark brown. Even the wing linings are dark, with the remaining underwing pale. Immatures are like females with pale bellies, males with a pale knob on the bill.

A sea duck, it nests on the tundra and inland lakes, migrating to the coasts in winter. Rather a shy species, it normally rides buoyantly, but can sink its body when alarmed.

White-winged and **Surf Scoters:** also mostly dark heavy sea-going ducks, but show white patches on the head or body. **Eiders:** heavy sea-going ducks, the males mostly black and white, the females brown with barred flanks. Other **Ducks** lack the heavy, stocky shape and long bulky bill.

♀

♂

Very dark duck overall, males showing obvious white forehead and nape patches, females with two whitish patches on the side of the head and nape.

Heavily built sea-going shape. Heavy triangular bill, strikingly white, yellow and red on the male. Underwings show gray, especially on female and immature birds which also have pale underparts.

A sea duck, it nests on the tundra and inland lakes, migrating to coastal wintering grounds. There it is usually seen well out from the shore.

Black- and **White-winged Scoters:** also mostly dark sea ducks, with a knob on the bill and/or pale cheek and throat, or white wing patches. **Eiders:** heavy sea ducks, males mostly black and white, females brown with barring. Other **Ducks** lack stocky shape and long, bulky bill.

Very dark duck overall, with the white secondaries showing as a patch towards the tail when swimming.

Heavily built sea-going shape. Underwings are pale. Apart from the secondaries patch, the male is mostly black, except for a white mark by the eye. The all brown female is similarly marked with faint patches.

A sea duck, it nests on the tundra and inland lakes, and is highly visible on migration to its coastal wintering grounds. Usually seen in flocks, this species dives for food, both animal and vegetable.

Black, Surf Scoters: mostly dark heavy sea ducks, plain wings and no white visible on body. **Eiders:** heavy sea ducks, males mostly black and white, females brown with barred flanks. Other **Ducks:** lack heavy shape, bulky bills. **Black, Pigeon Guillemots:** different profiles, white patch in middle.

51

♀

♂

Pale-backed and dark-breasted, with a long triangular forehead and bill.

Pale flanks and dark bill shared by both sexes. The male has a chestnut head and neck, and a black breast and undertail. The female and male during molt have a brown head, neck and breast.

A diving duck, it eats mostly vegetable matter with some worms, frogs etc. Seen in large flocks on open water, such as lakes and marshes. Very widespread, it breeds as far north as Alaska, wintering in Mexico and the south.

Both **Scaups:** shorter pale bills, head shapes more rounded.
Eiders and **Scoters:** much heavier sea-going shape. Other **Ducks** lack the long triangular forehead and bill.

○♂

●♀

●♂

White body. Plain dark wings above and below.

Male has dark head, neck and breast in summer, turning pale or white by winter. Face stays whitish. Male also has conspicuous long tail. Female is similarly marked, but is generally paler in winter, darker in summer.

A sea duck, this species nests on the tundra lakes, wintering on the Great Lakes and coastlines. Common and visible, Oldsquaws also draw attention to themselves with their noisy calls and their distinctive swinging flight.

Bufflehead: similar colors, but much smaller with white wing patches. **Goldeneyes:** males are white-bodied but show clear white speculum in flight.

Heavy sea-going duck, with a large rounded head and straight bill, the male being black-backed and white-breasted.

The adult male is black, white, pale peach on the breast, with pale blue crown and nape, an obvious orange frontal shield and red bill. The female is all brown with "herringbone" bars on flanks, and shows a conspicuous "grin" line.

Found only in the north, it breeds on the Arctic tundra, wintering in small numbers on both east and west coastlines, where it is normally a deep-water duck. The male coos and the female groans, quite like the Common Eider.

Common Eider males have white backs. Both sexes have oversized triangular heads, females showing darkly barred flanks. **Scoters:** heavy sea ducks, dark plain colors, males mostly black, females mostly brown. Other **Ducks** lack heavy stocky shape and long, bulky bills.

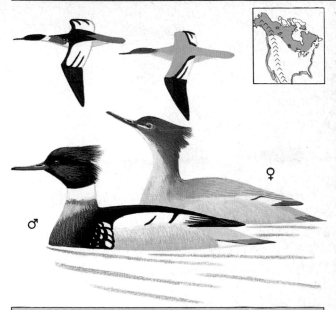

Long, slim red bill. Both sexes have twin-pronged crests. Female's chin and front of throat are pale.

Male: glossy green head, white collar and rufous streaked breast. Black above. Female: gray above with a rust colored head. Both sexes have gray wings and tail with pale underwing and belly.

This species nests in wooded areas around northern lakes, but in winter migrates and may be seen on any body of water, fresh or salt, including sea coasts. Distinctive all-in-a-line (bill, head, body, tail) flight posture.

Other **Ducks** do not share long slim bill.

55

Heavy sea-going duck with an oversized triangular head, the male with a white back.

The male is uniquely colored black, white, pale peach on the breast and delicate green on the nape. The female is all brown with dark barred flanks and a smooth back profile. Both sexes have a long flat forehead.

Found only in the north, it breeds on the Arctic tundra, and winters in large flocks along rocky shorelines. The comic "aah-ooor" call of the males often locates unseen birds at sea. On land the rolling waddle is also distinctive.

King Eider male has a black back. The female has a more rounded head, and "herringbone" barring on the flanks. **Scoters:** heavy sea-going ducks, dark plain colors, males nearly all black, females nearly all brown. Other **Ducks** lack the heavy, stocky shape and long, bulky bills.

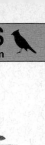

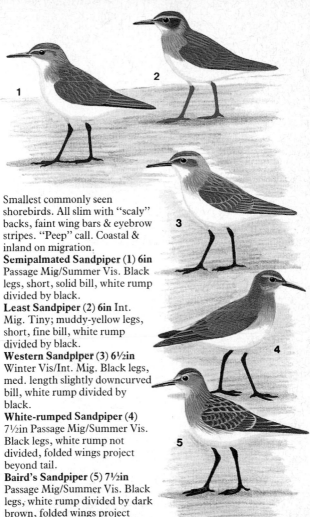

Smallest commonly seen
shorebirds. All slim with "scaly"
backs, faint wing bars & eyebrow
stripes. "Peep" call. Coastal &
inland on migration.

Semipalmated Sandpiper (1) 6in
Passage Mig/Summer Vis. Black
legs, short, solid bill, white rump
divided by black.

Least Sandpiper (2) 6in Int.
Mig. Tiny; muddy-yellow legs,
short, fine bill, white rump
divided by black.

Western Sandpiper (3) 6½in
Winter Vis/Int. Mig. Black legs,
med. length slightly downcurved
bill, white rump divided by
black.

White-rumped Sandpiper (4)
7½in Passage Mig/Summer Vis.
Black legs, white rump not
divided, folded wings project
beyond tail.

Baird's Sandpiper (5) 7½in
Passage Mig/Summer Vis. Black
legs, white rump divided by dark
brown, folded wings project
beyond tail.

♂

△

Thin bill, incomplete breast band, pale back, black legs.

The bill is dark, as are the ear coverts and a band across the crown. The wings show a white wing bar. The sides of the rump and tail are white, as is all the remaining plumage. Juveniles show pale colors for dark bands.

Less common nowadays, it breeds mainly on sandy beaches, often mixed in with other plovers. It calls a soft "kerweet." In winter it is a partial migrant, many birds being seen around the Gulf and on the west coast.

Piping Plover: stubby bill, breast band sometimes complete, orange legs. **Wilson's** and **Semipalmated Plovers** have medium brown backs and complete breast bands.

Stubby bill, complete breast band, medium brown back, orange legs.

The bill is orange, tipped black. Crown and nape match the back, forehead matches breast band, remaining plumage is white. Sexes are alike. Juveniles have gray legs. Colors fade a little in winter but bill darkens.

This species breeds in the far north. Widespread during migration, it may be seen throughout the continent. Wintering grounds are mostly on mud flats, sand bars and beaches.

Wilson's Plover: heavy billed, pinkish legs. **Piping Plover:** breast band sometimes complete (only on breeding birds,) pale back. **Snowy Plover:** thin bill, incomplete breast band, pale back, black legs.

PIPING PLOVER
Resident/Internal Migrant

7¼in

♂

Stubby bill, breast band **sometimes complete (but only on breeding birds), pale back, orange legs.**

The bill is orange, tipped black. The crown has a dark band in summer only. White shows on collar, across rump before a dark tail, as a wing bar, and on all underparts. Juveniles have pale colors for dark bands, and a dark bill.

Named for its characteristic "peep-lo" call, this species nests in Canada, around the Great Lakes, and on sandy beaches along our east coasts. It winters in the south, into Mexico, and South America.

Snowy Plover: thin bill, incomplete breast band, black legs.
Wilson's Plover: heavy-billed, broad complete breast band, medium brown back and pinkish legs. **Semipalmated Plover:** medium brown back, complete breast band.

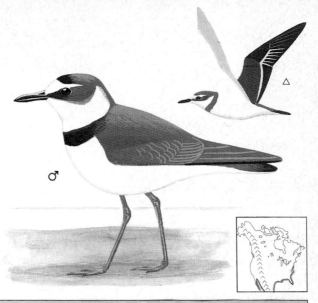

Heavy bill, broad complete breast band, gray-brown back, pinkish legs.

Black bill. Black crown band, and breast bar on the breeding male. Females have brown bands when breeding. All these colors fade in winter, as with juveniles. All have a short white wing bar and a divided white rump.

Breeding on sandy beaches and islands along eastern coast, it is often located by its brief "whit" call. In winter it is a partial migrant only, some birds staying in Florida rather than moving across the Gulf.

Semipalmated Plover: stubby bill, thinner breast band, orange legs. **Piping Plover:** stubby bill, breast band sometimes complete (only on breeding birds,) pale back, orange legs. **Snowy Plover:** thin bill, incomplete breast band, pale back, black legs.

61

Elegant little seabird, often "spinning" on the water, white-chinned in summer, and retaining striped back in winter.

"Needle"-bill. Breeding adults red on sides of neck, upper breast. Dark upperparts striped with buff. Underparts are white. Winter plumage is gray and white, a black mark prominent through the eye. Wing stripe shows in flight.

Breeds high on the tundra, and is mostly seen on passage southwards, usually in coastal locations or at sea. It "spins" to disturb food, and is a highly active swimming feeder. It winters at sea.

Red Phalarope: red-chinned in summer, plain gray-backed in winter, with the bill stouter than Red-necked. **Fork-tailed Storm-Petrel:** tube-nosed seabird, with the long tail forked. **Sanderling:** remarkable scuttling run at water's edge, back and forth with the waves.

Remarkable scuttling run at water's edge, back and forth with the waves

Juveniles and molting adults are scaly-backed, in contrast to the plain pale gray of the winter adult. In summer the whole front half of the bird becomes uniformly rust colored.

In summer it breeds on the Arctic tundra. In winter, seen around the Great Lakes and on sandy beaches all around shorelines, feeding in between the waves. This high activity makes the species distinctive.

No other shorebirds feed running with the waves, but note **Red Knot:** larger. Pale wings with poorly defined wing stripe. (Winter) **Dunlin:** downcurved bill. Small **"Peep" Sandpipers:** wing stripes poorly defined.

RED PHALAROPE
Passage Migrant/Winter Visitor   8½in

Elegant little seabird, often "spinning" on the water, red-chinned in summer and plain gray-backed in winter.

Has shortest and thickest bill of the Phalaropes. Breeding adults have foreneck and underparts red. Face is white. Winter plumage is gray and white, a black mark prominent through the eye. A white wing stripe shows in flight.

Breeds high on the tundra, and is mostly seen on passage southwards, mainly along the Pacific coast. It "spins" to disturb food and is a highly active swimming feeder, sometimes upending. It winters at sea.

Red-necked Phalarope: white-chinned in summer, retaining its striped back in winter, with a slender bill. **Fork-tailed Storm-Petrel:** tube-nosed seabird, with the long tail forked. **Sanderling:** remarkable scuttling run at water's edge, back and forth with the waves.

West coast shorebird, with long, slightly downcurved bill, and short yellowish legs. (Summer) black patch on lower breast. (Winter) plain slate-gray head.

Stocky build. Bill is greenish yellow at base. Rufous crown and white eyebrow, brown scaly back, in summer only. In winter, breast heavily streaked fading to white belly. White wing bar and divided white rump visible in flight.

Breeding coastally in the far northwest, this species migrates down west coast, wintering around rocky locations. Gregarious, often with Ruddy Turnstones.

(Winter) **Purple Sandpiper:** similar but east coast only. **Dunlin:** black legs. (Summer) black belly. (Winter) **Red Knot:** larger, stockier. Straight bill. **Surfbird, Turnstones:** short bills, stout shapes. **"Peep" Sandpipers:** small. Slim build, comparatively short bills, "scaly" backs.

Medium length slightly downcurved bill, short yellow legs, white rump divided, East coast species. (Summer) heavily streaked. (Winter) dark gray head.

Stocky build. Bill is orange-yellow at base. Rufous crown and white eyebrow, brown scaly back in summer only. In winter breast is heavily streaked, fading to white belly. White wing bar and divided white rump visible in flight.

Breeding in the far north, often away from coasts, it migrates down eastern coast, wintering around rocky locations. Gregarious, often with Ruddy Turnstones.

(Winter) **Rock Sandpiper:** similar but west coast species. **Dunlin:** black legs. (Summer) black belly. (Winter) **Red Knot:** larger, stockier. Straight bill. **Surfbird, Turnstones:** short bills. Stout shapes. **"Peep" Sandpipers:** small, slim build, comparatively short bills, "scaly" backs.

Long, slightly downcurved bill. Black legs. (Summer) black belly. (Winter) unpatterned gray-brown back.

Stocky build. In summer, chestnut and black upperparts. In winter, pale gray breast streaks on white underparts. Juveniles rusty above, streaked below. In flight, note clear wing bar and white rump divided by black.

Arctic breeder. On migration and in winter, seen at mud flats, small pools, beaches. Mannerisms include a "stitching" feeding motion, round-shouldered appearance. Gregarious, it disturbs in wheeling flocks with shrill notes.

(Summer) **Rock Sandpiper:** black patch on lower breast. Yellowish legs. (Winter) **Rock, Purple Sandpipers:** yellowish legs. **Red Knot:** straight bill. Pale back. Greenish legs. Small **"Peep" Sandpipers:** size, slim build, comparatively short bills, "scaly" backs.

67

Quite distinctive black, white and ruddy brown wing pattern, and black and white head pattern. Colors fade in winter but the markings remain recognizable.

Described as "harlequin" patterned with a "tortoiseshell" back plumage, other markings of this striking bird are a white belly and breast, black bib, and very obvious orange legs. A stocky shorebird with a short bill. Sexes alike.

It breeds on the Arctic tundra, and is seen on passage or as a winter visitor. Jerky actions and short skittering runs are broken by pauses to feed, turning over stones and shells. Seen on rocky shorelines, and on mud flats.

Black Turnstone: at rest, markings are quite different, but beware wing pattern in flight. This is a darker version of the Ruddy Turnstone, lacking the ruddy brown colors.

Whole upper body very dark, with quite distinctive pied back, and wing pattern prominent in flight.

Slim dark bill, blackish legs. In breeding plumage, lores and eyebrow are white on otherwise black upperparts. In winter, all upperparts become dark gray. Belly and undertail pure white at all times.

Breeding coastally in the far northwest, it migrates south along western coastline, favoring rocky locations. Jerky actions between feeding alert the observer, as the plumage otherwise blends into the background.

Ruddy Turnstone: similar markings in flight, but ruddy brown colors, black bib. Winter **Surfbird:** plain dark upperparts, prominent white rump, spotted belly. Winter **Rock, Purple Sandpipers:** single white wing bars and divided rumps in flight, longish downcurved bills, yellowish legs.

69

Short bill, short yellow legs. Plain back and prominent white rump visible in flight.

Bill is pale at base. Breeding birds have heavily mottled backs. Winter plumage alters to plain gray upperparts with a spotted white belly. Single strong white wing bars are clear in flight.

Breeding on the far northwestern mountainous tundra, it migrates south along western coastlines, favoring rocky locations. Often seen in groups, it feeds inconspicuously among the rocks, blending into the background.

Black and **Ruddy Turnstones:** white down back and on wings provides distinctive pied pattern in flight. **Rock** and **Purple Sandpipers:** longish downcurved bills. In flight, white rumps are divided.

Extremely gregarious. A stout, straight-billed shorebird with (winter) pale gray back and (summer) rusty coloring. In flight note the pale (speckled) undivided rump.

Bill is short in proportion to overall size of bird. Pale wing bar visible in flight, as is pale rump and tail. Winter and juvenile's plumage is gray above, nearly white underparts, with some streaking on the upper breast.

An Arctic breeder, it is normally seen on migration, or wintering in large numbers feeding on mud flats, beaches. Often associated with other shorebirds, notably Dowitchers. Call-note is "nut," flight-call "twit-it."

(Winter) **Dunlin**, **Rock** and **Purple Sandpipers:** smaller. Longish downcurved bills. In flight, rumps clearly divided. **Dowitchers:** white wedge up the dark backs in flight. **Wandering Tattler:** dark rumped in flight. **Surfbird**, **Turnstones:** short bills, pied back and wing patterns in flight.

71

A bulky silvery gray shorebird with a white rump visible in flight.

In breeding plumage face, breast and belly are black. Forehead, crown, nape, sides of breast, form a white stripe. In winter, whole bird appears gray, paler below. Black wing pits and a bold white wing stripe are visible in flight.

Breeds on the Arctic tundra. Winters coastally around beaches, or marshy ground, mud flats. Not gregarious, usually seen singly or in small numbers. Wary, normally seen at distance, its large size is distinctive.

None.

Plain dark gray upperparts, which include the rump, tail, and underwing.

Blackish bill. The head shows a dark eye stripe below a white eyebrow stripe. Breeding birds have barred underparts. Other plumages show gray on the breast and flanks with the belly white. Legs are muddy-yellow.

Breeding in the far northwest around streams, these birds winter on our southwestern rocky coasts. Migration is mostly coastal. Peculiar bobbing motion when feeding. May prefer to crouch when disturbed, rather than fly.

Willet (winter): black and white wings. Larger. **Yellowlegs** and **Dowitchers** (winter): white rump/wedge up back. Other Shorebirds which show grayish upperparts, normally in winter, are mostly smaller with white wing bars and white or whitish rumps or rump edges.

Long bills, and white wedges up the dark backs. Long-billed
(1;) Short-billed (2.)

All brown birds, heavily flecked, streaked and barred with black.
Bellies less marked. Prominent pale eyebrows. In breeding
plumages the brown is red-brown, turning gray-brown in winter.
The juveniles are illustrated.

Usually observed on migration, these birds are seen at shallow
water locations, feeding with a "stitching" action. Easily
disturbed, they give alarm calls, "tu, tu, tu" for the Short-billed,
"keek" for the Long-billed.

Red Knot: stout, dark back, pale rump. **Marbled Godwit:** far
larger, plain brown back, slightly upturned bill. **Wandering
Tattler** (winter): plain dark back, rump. **Yellowlegs:** orange-
yellow legs. **Willet:** black and white wings. Other gray or brown
Shorebirds: mostly smaller, lack wedge up back.

Long legs are bright orange-yellow. Medium length and fairly long bills respectively. Greater (1;) Lesser (2.)

Brown backs flecked with black in breeding plumages, and with white in juveniles. Pale underparts, heavily streaked on heads, necks, breasts. White rumps, pale tails, with some streaking on the belly of the Greater.

Nesting on the tundra, these species winter on our southern coasts, the Greater being more widespread. The Greater's call is a sequence of three "yew" notes, the Lesser's is fainter and usually only one or two "yew"s.

Willet: black and white wings, bluish gray legs. **Wandering Tattler:** plain dark gray upperparts including rump and tail. Muddy-yellow legs. **Dowitchers:** white wedge up backs. Muddy-green legs.

75

Large black-and-white-winged wading bird with a straight bill and bluish gray legs.

Nondescript gray-brown above, paler below. Summer breeding plumage shows streaking and barring. Bill is straight, fairly heavy and fairly long. Juveniles show a brown "scaly" back.

Rather local but numerous where it is found. Noisy and prominent, this species prefers marshes, shores and wet meadows. In winter it is restricted to coastal regions. The name is derived from its call, "pill-will-willet."

Wandering Tattler, Greater and **Lesser Yellowlegs, Short-** and **Long-billed Dowitchers:** smaller with plain dark wings. Other Shorebirds with black and white wings are all smaller.

Long, downcurved bill and strongly striped crown.

The body is mainly gray-brown with the underparts paler than the back and the belly off-white. There is also an eye stripe in addition to those over the crown. Gray legs.

The species spends the summer breeding on the tundra, migrating to more southerly coasts where it may be seen in wet fields, marshes, mud flats and beaches. A typical call is a sequence of whistles.

Long-billed Curlew: very long, downcurved bill. **Marbled Godwit:** long, slightly upturned bill. Similar size. **White Ibis:** bright red legs. Areas of white increase to adult's all white plumage. Other Shorebirds are nearly all smaller and have straighter and shorter bills.

Long, thick, straight bill (bright orange in adults.)

Dark brown back, wings and tail, black head and neck, contrast with pure white underparts, rump and very prominent wing patches. Legs are pink, grayer on juveniles. Juveniles are scaly-backed, and the bill is a dull color.

Gregarious, this noisy species is seen in large flocks along beaches and mud flats. Easily disturbed, their penetrating "kleep" calls sound the alarm. The bill is used to break open shellfish.

None.

Large shorebird, with a long slightly upturned bill.

The whole body is buff brown, blended with dark brown above and barred below. The bill is orange-brown at the base, shading to a dark tip. The legs are gray.

This large bird uses its long legs and long bill to wade and feed in pools and lake margins to a greater depth than many other shorebirds. It nests mainly in the Great Plains close to water, migrating to the coasts in winter.

Whimbrel, Long-billed Curlew: markedly downcurved bills.
Willet, Greater and **Lesser Yellowlegs, Wandering Tattler, Short-** and **Long-billed Dowitchers:** much smaller with shorter straight bills.

Very long, downcurved bill. Cinnamon-brown back.

The body is mainly cinnamon-brown with the underparts notably darker and ruddier than the Whimbrel, but colors fade a little in winter. The wing pits are cinnamon. Gray legs.

Seen more inland than the Whimbrel, these curlew breed on dry uplands as well as wet locations. In winter they are seen widely, from farmland to freshwater, saltwater margins, marshes and mud flats. The call is an eerie "cur-lee."

Whimbrel: long downcurved bill, strongly striped crown.
Marbled Godwit: long, slightly upturned bill. Smaller. **White Ibis:** bright red legs. Areas of white increase to all white adult. Other Shorebirds are nearly all smaller and have shorter and straighter bills.

Adults show pointed streamers. Immatures and juveniles have shorter, but still pointed, streamers.

Shallower, more pointed wings than skuas. Dark phase adults are brown overall, black cap, some white in primaries. Light phase adults show yellowish throat, some breast bar, pale below. Juveniles show barring below.

Breeds on Arctic tundra, visiting coasts in the winter. A falcon-like flier with a dashing action, it will pursue birds to force them to disgorge; also eats carrion.

Long-tailed Jaegers: double streamers, shorter and blunter in young birds. **Pomarine Jaegers:** "spoon" twisted streamers, shorter and blunter in young birds. **Skuas:** heavier build, negligible streamers, bold wing patches very prominent. **Great** and **Cory's Shearwaters:** tube-nosed.

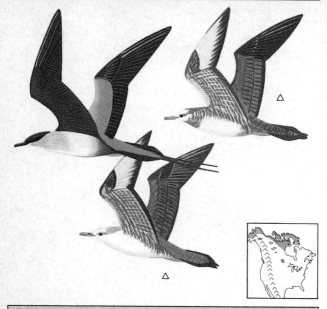

Adults show remarkable long double tail streamers. Immatures and juveniles have shorter blunter streamers.

Trim build. Shallower, more pointed wings than skuas. Adults show gray-brown back, yellowish white throat and collar, whitish below (no breast bar.) Juveniles show barring below, but are notoriously variable.

Breeds on Arctic tundra, visiting coasts on passage to south Atlantic and Pacific. Shows a rather aimless, tilting flight, much weaker than other jaegers, is less inclined to pursue other species, more inclined to take carrion.

Immature and Juvenile **Pomarine Jaeger:** heavier build, white wing bar in upperwing primaries. Adult **Pomarine** and **Parasitic Jaegers:** distinctive and shorter tail streamers. **Skuas:** heavier build, negligible streamers, bold wing patches very prominent. **Great** and **Cory's Shearwaters:** tube-nosed.

Adults show remarkable long "spoon" twisted tail streamers. Immatures and juveniles have shorter blunter streamers.

Strong build. Shallower, more pointed wings than skuas. Dark phase adults are brown overall, with a black cap, some white in primaries. Light phases show yellowish throat, dark breast bar, paler below. All juveniles heavily barred below.

Breeds on Arctic tundra, visiting coasts in winter. Powerful, with a deliberate slow flight, it will pursue birds to force them to disgorge. It also eats carrion and will follow ships.

Immature and juvenile **Long-tailed Jaeger:** lighter build, negligible white in upperwing primaries. **Parasitic Jaeger:** two pointed streamers, shorter in younger birds. **Skuas:** heavier build, negligible streamers, bold wing patches very prominent. **Great** and **Cory's Shearwaters:** tube-nosed.

Very heavily built, mostly dark brown seabird, bold white wing patches in primaries, and variable shades of gray (light or dark phase) around neck and in underparts.

Bullnecked, with a hooked beak and deep wings. The darkest phase birds usually show a pale area at the base of the bill, lighter phases contrasting with the Great Skua by their gray areas. Juveniles similar.

Breeds on the Antarctic continent, visiting our coasts in the summer. Powerful, with a strong direct flight, it will pursue birds to force them to disgorge. It also eats carrion and will follow ships.

Great Skua: mostly rufous brown, with neck and underparts essentially the same color as the head, back and wings. **Jaegers** have noticeably lighter build and shallower, more pointed wings. The adults also have very distinctive central tail feathers.

Very heavily built, mostly rufous brown seabird, with bold white wing patches in the primaries.

Bullneck, hooked beak and deep wings distinguish Skuas from other seabirds. The back has golden brown flecks, with the cap and wings rather darker. Juveniles are very similar.

Breeds widely around the north Atlantic, visiting east coast in winter. The larger skua, powerful, with a strong direct flight, it will pursue birds to force them to disgorge. It also eats carrion and will follow ships.

South Polar Skua: brown colors are darker and grayer. The variable phases show varying amounts of gray around the neck and on the underparts. **Jaegers** have a noticeably lighter build and shallower, more pointed wings. The adults also have very distinctive central tail feathers.

**Smallest tern, with a forked tail, white forehead. Breeding
adults have yellow bills.**

Yellow bill has black tip. Black-capped, pale gray above, white
below. Juveniles, immatures and winter adults have blackish or
black bills, and show a dark shoulder bar. Breeding adults have
black outer primaries.

Nests in colonies on coastal beaches, and on sand bars and
estuaries inland. As it is so small, the flight is very buoyant, and
the wingbeats very fast. Extremely aggressive for its size.

Other **Terns:** much larger. Small **Gulls** are larger and lack forked
tail.

A small black-billed gull, summer adults have a black hood, and white wedge at wing tips.

Adult: back and most of wings gray, white body, red legs. From fall, hood replaced by dark ear spot. Immatures lack full hood, have brown bar on innerwing, some of white wedge, black tail band. Adult plumage in second year.

Buoyant in flight like terns, these active noisy gulls breed across Canada on the lakes. They then migrate to more southerly coastlines and especially the Great Lakes. Call of "churr" and chattering notes.

Laughing Gull: adults hooded in summer, but all ages have wings tipped with solid black. Larger. Other **Gulls:** not hooded, larger, lack the wedge of white at the wing tip. **Terns** have cleft or forked tails, and are black-capped rather than black-headed.

87

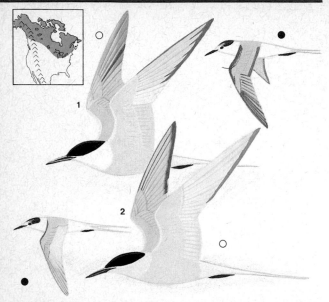

(Adults) deeply forked tails. Red bills and feet. Primaries have dark margins, rather more "filled in" on the Common Tern (1.) (Juveniles/Immatures) black all around nape.

Black cap. Bill black tipped on Common Tern. Mid-gray above, whitish below. Juveniles, immatures, winter adults show pinkish or black bills, and a dark shoulder bar lacking on Forster's Tern. Note Common Tern's black primary.

Exclusively associated with water, they feed by plunge-diving for fish. Flight is buoyant and bounding. These common summer visitors breed in huge colonies, Arctic Terns (2) more northerly, returning to the Antarctic in winter.

Forster's Tern: (Adult) orange-red bill and feet. Primaries paler than rest of wing. (Juveniles/Immatures) black eye patch not around nape. **Gull-billed** and **Sandwich Terns** have black bills, feet. Small **Gulls**, inc. **Kittiwake:** heavier build, blunt tails, black on wing tips.

(Adult) **Deeply forked tail. Orange-red bill and feet. Primaries paler gray than remainder of wing.** (Juveniles/Immatures) **Black eye patch does not go around the nape.**

Black-capped, orange-red bill has black tip. Pale gray above and very white below. Juveniles, immatures and winter adults show pinkish or black bills, and lack the shoulder bar which is seen on Common and Arctic Terns.

Widely spread, including a resident area on the Gulf Coast, Forster's Terns nest colonially in marshy habitats, becoming coastal in winter. Like other terns, they plunge-dive for fish, from a buoyant and bounding flight.

Common, **Arctic Terns:** (Adults) red bills, feet. Primaries have dark margins, "filled in" on Common Tern. (Juveniles/ Immatures) black all around nape. **Gull-billed**, **Sandwich Terns:** black bills, feet. Small **Gulls**, inc. **Kittiwake:** heavier build, blunt tails, black on wing tips.

Stout black gull-like bill, black feet. Markedly notched tail.

Stocky for a tern. In summer, it shows a black cap and nape, pale gray above and white elsewhere. In winter the head becomes white with gray flecks and a patch around the eye. Juveniles show brownish gray.

Common where it is found, but restricted to coastal locations in the east and extreme southwest, returning mainly to South America in winter. Hawks for insects more than plunge-dives, with a distinctly gull-like flight.

Sandwich Tern: long black bill. Adults have a deeply forked tail, are crested, and the bill is tipped with yellow. All other adult **Terns** have red or yellow bills. All small **Gulls** have black on the wing tips and blunt tails.

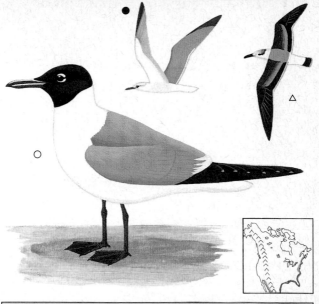

Adults have dark gray wings tipped with solid black.

The back is dark gray, the feet are black. In summer this species is black-headed with a red bill, otherwise white. In winter the head is a dirty white and the bill black. Immatures are varying browns with solid black-tipped wings.

The name is due to its harsh cry. A common coastal bird, predominantly of the east coast, it ventures inland infrequently.

Black-legged Kittiwake: black legs. Pale gray wings tipped solid black, no black head. **Bonaparte's Gull:** smaller, pale gray back, red legs. **Mew** and **Ring-billed Gulls:** pale gray back, white in black wing tips. Other **Gulls:** notably larger. **Terns:** slimmer, cleft or forked tails, black-capped.

Adults have yellow-green legs, and slim yellow bills without any markings (immatures' are black-tipped).

Gray back and wings, black-tipped with white spots. Head, tail, underparts are white, with the head speckled brown in winter. Immatures variously brown with dark-tipped bills for two years. Brown head, bill shape and build identifies.

Breeding throughout western Canada, it migrates south along the west coast to the Mexican border in winter. Common on beaches, mud flats and most locations where food may be scavenged.

Ring-billed Gull: adults have yellow bill entirely encircled by a black ring. **California Gull:** larger. Adults have a yellow bill with both red and black spots. **Herring** and **Thayer's Gulls:** pink legs. **Black-legged Kittiwake:** black legs.

Pale gray wings tipped with solid black. Black legs.

The bill is unmarked yellow. The back and upperwings are gray. It is otherwise white. Immature birds have a black half collar, ear spot, tail band, and a very distinctive "W" across the wings. The tail may appear slightly cleft.

A truly sea-going bird, only seen on land nesting in colonies on cliffs. It breeds in the far north and is normally seen off coasts in winter. Flight is buoyant and bounding. Call is "kitti-waake."

Laughing Gull: adults have dark gray wings tipped solid black. Black hood in summer. **Bonaparte's Gull:** white wedge at wing tips. Black bill, red legs. Other **Gulls** with black wing tips have white spots inset. **Terns:** markedly cleft or forked tails, usually black-capped.

93

Adults have a deeply forked tail, are crested, and the long black bill is tipped with yellow.

Black legs. Pale gray above, white below. Black-capped in summer, this fades in winter to leave the forehead white and crown streaked. Juveniles and Immatures may lack yellow bill tip, and show blackish bars on back and tail.

Found on the east coast, this comic-looking tern is more elegant than the Gull-billed Terns, plunge-diving for fish off sandy beach and island breeding colonies. Mostly winters off South America, except for Gulf populations.

Gull-billed Tern: stout black gull-like bill. Tail merely notched. All other adult **Terns** have red or yellow bills. All small **Gulls** have a heavier build, blunt tails and black on wing tips.

Adults have yellow legs. The yellow bill is entirely encircled by a black ring.

Gray back and wings, black-tipped with white spots. Head, tail, underparts are white, with the head speckled brown in winter. Immatures show varying brown plumages, dark bills, for two years. The light build identifies with practice.

An abundant species. Although common in coastal regions, it is also found inland around water, plowed fields and dumps, with the winter range more southerly than the central breeding habitat.

Mew Gull: adults have yellow legs, and delicate yellow bill without any markings (immature's black-tipped). **California Gull:** larger. Adults have a yellow bill with red and black spots. **Herring** and **Thayer's Gulls:** pink legs. **Black-legged Kittiwake:** black legs.

Lower bill larger than upper, for remarkable skimming fishing technique.

The huge red bill is black-tipped. Upperparts are black including the center of the tail. Underparts are white as are the wing's trailing edges. The wings are extremely long and pointed. Juveniles have brown and white in the wings.

This largely resident coastal species is quite unique in its fishing technique. It flies buoyantly, then descends to level flight just above the water with the lower bill slicing the water, until it snaps shut on a fish.

None.

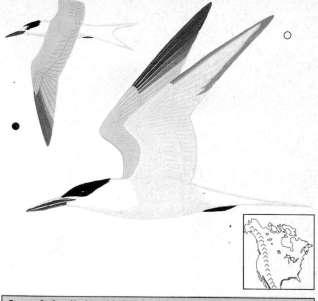

Large fork-tailed seabird with a large plain orange-red bill.

Fairly heavy, but sleeker than gulls, with typical tern's pointed wings. Black-capped, upperparts pale gray, underparts white, dark in wing tips. Legs black. Non-breeders and late summer birds lack full black cap.

Breeding in colonies around Central American coastlines, it may be seen further north in winter months. It favors sandy beaches and banks, and may be seen in strong flight or plunge-diving for fish.

Caspian Tern: bill is redder and heavier with a black tip. Tail is notched. Other red-billed **Terns** are much smaller. **Gulls** have a different build, blunt tails and more rounded wings.

97

Large notch-tailed seabird, with a heavy red bill black at the tip.

Heavily built, different in proportion to gulls, with typical tern's pointed wings. Black-capped, upperparts pale gray, underparts white, a dark panel under the wing tips. Legs black. Non-breeding plumages similar.

Widespread, but only common locally, it breeds across the continent in marsh, inland lake, and coastal habitats. Large, its flight is less bounding than smaller terns, and it plunge-dives from a greater height.

Royal Tern: fork-tailed seabirds with a large plain orange-red bill. Other red-billed **Terns** are much smaller. **Gulls** have a different build, blunt tails and more rounded wings.

Adults have yellow-green legs and a yellow bill with both a red spot and a small black spot.

Adult has gray back and wings, tipped black and white, white tail, underparts and head. The head has brown speckles in winter. Juveniles and immatures show varying brown plumages for three years.

Common in the west, this species breeds inland, migrating to the west coast in winter, only the occasional straggler reaching the east coast. It is found on beaches, coasts, rivers and even in cities.

Adult **Ring-billed Gull:** yellow legs, yellow bill entirely encircled by black ring. **Herring, Thayer's, Glaucous-winged Gulls:** pink legs. **Mew Gull:** smaller, with delicate yellow unmarked bill.

99

Adults have mid-gray back, black-tipped wings, pink legs, pale eye.

Adults: gray wings, white head, tail and underparts. Heavy yellow bill with red spot. In winter, neck and breast become speckled brown. Immatures show varying brown plumages and dark bills for three years. Very uniformly dark.

Although common in coastal regions, this abundant species is seen inland as well. A raucous scavenger, frequently found at dumps.

Adult **Thayer's Gull**: smaller area of dark gray in wing tips, dark eye. Adult **Mew**, **Ring-billed**, **California Gulls**: smaller. Yellow legs. **Glaucous**, **Iceland** and **Glaucous-winged Gulls**: lack large black area in primaries. Palest **Western Gulls** have dark gray backs and wings.

Adults have gray back, dark gray in wing tips, pink legs, dark eye.

Adults: gray wings, white head, tail and underparts. Yellow bill has red spot. In winter, neck and breast become speckled brown. Immatures show varying brown plumages and dark bills for three years.

Breeding high on the tundra, this species (previously considered to be a form of the Herring Gull,) winters mostly down the west coast. Attends ships, garbage dumps.

Herring Gull: greater area of black wing tip, pale eye. **Glaucous**, **Iceland Gulls:** wing tips are white, or unmarked, and the gray-tipped form of Iceland Gull is an eastern species. **Glaucous-winged**, **California**, **Ring-billed** and **Mew Gulls:** yellow legs.

Large gulls with very pale gray/white backs and wings. Wing tips are white (pale gray in some forms of Iceland Gull.) **Glaucous (1;) Iceland (2.)**

Pink legs. Adults have red-spotted yellow bills, pale eyes. The remaining plumage is white. Immatures are a very pale mottled brown, with dark on the bills for three years. The Iceland Gull has the more rounded head and smaller bill.

Both breed in the Arctic, Glaucous Gull winters down both coasts, but Iceland Gull is seen only on the east. The heavy chested Glaucous Gull is lumbering in flight, the Iceland Gull has a quicker more buoyant wing action.

Thayer's Gull: very similar to gray-tipped form of Iceland Gull, but restricted to west. Dark eyed. **Glaucous-winged Gull:** a western species, gray wing tips have white spots inset. Dark eyed. All other gray-backed **Gulls** have black in wing tips.

Adults have black (very dark gray) backs. **Pink legs.**

Large gulls. Head, neck, underparts are white. Wing color same as back. Bills are yellow, red-spotted. Immatures have varying brown plumages and dark on bills for three years.

Eastern and western coastal species respectively. True coastal species. Do not frequently wander inland.

Other **Gulls** have pale gray backs, except the **Laughing Gull** which has a dark gray back, but is far smaller with black legs.

Large gull with pale gray back and wings. Wing tips are the same color with white spots inset. A western species.

Pink legs. Adults have yellow bills with red spots, and a dark eye. The remaining plumage is white. Immature birds are varying browns with dark on bills for three years.

Numerous along our western coasts, this species breeds in Canada and Alaska, migrating south in winter. Very much a coastal species, it is usually seen around harbors and garbage dumps. Flight is powerful and direct.

Iceland Gull: very similar but an eastern species. **Thayer's Gull:** dark gray in wing tips. Dark eyed. **Glaucous Gull:** white wing tips. All other gray-backed **Gulls** have black in wing tips.

Plump, starling-sized seabird, with a stubby bill in all seasons.
Whirring flight.

Bill is black. Black above and white below like many auks, with
white flecks on the back, but these are only visible at close range.
In winter the throat, chin, and parts of the neck turn white.
Young birds show some brown.

The smallest east coast auk, this dumpy little bird appears
neckless and tailless, flying with extremely rapid whirring wing
beats. An abundant species, it breeds in the high Arctic, wintering
out in the north Atlantic.

Murrelets and **Cassin's Auklet:** similar profile, most are larger,
but all are found on the west coast. Winter **Atlantic Puffin:** larger
size could be overlooked at sea, but even the winter bill is
noticeably bigger.

CASSIN'S AUKLET
Resident/Internal Migrant   8½in

A small, plump, gray seabird. The pale base of the lower
mandible shows as a light spot on a dark bill.

The belly is pale, although this is only visible in flight. Pale gray
streak behind eye, and white crescent over eye, may be visible at
close range. Note the rounded wing tips. Sexes are alike. Juveniles
have a paler throat.

Widespread and seen in large flocks, this species breeds on islands
all along western coastline. Normally seen at sea circling when
disturbed, it has a whirring direct flight.

Summer **Marbled Murrelet:** brown and mottled, much darker
above. Medium, pointed bill. **Rhinoceros Auklet:** far larger,
heavy pale bill with "horn" in summer. Juvenile **Tufted Puffin:**
far larger, red feet, heavy bill. **Dovekie:** similar size and shape,
only found in the Atlantic.

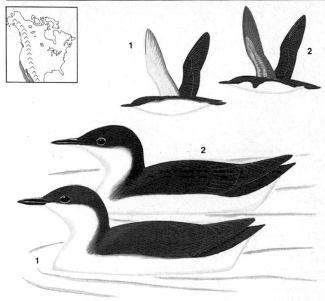

Clear-cut plain black above white below plumage (winter and summer,) slim bills and southerly range. Whirring flight. Xantu's (1;) Craveri's (2.)

All ages, sexes, and seasonal plumages are alike. The best distinction is that Xantu's Murrelet has a white underwing, Craveri's a gray underwing. However this may prove hard to see due to the rapid wingbeats.

Not especially common, and restricted to southwestern and Mexican coastline, these species normally breed on islands. At sea, they sit low in the water, with the head typically held uptilted.

Winter **Marbled Murrelet:** prominent white markings down back. **Ancient Murrelet:** black head contrasts with blue-gray back. Short pale bill, and black bib (summer adult.)

MARBLED MURRELET
Resident/Internal Migrant   9¾in

(Summer) **Brown and mottled, much darker above.** (Winter)
Prominent white markings down back (scapulars.)

Medium length black pointed bill. Summer plumage as described
above. Winter colors change to gray-black above, and white below
with an incomplete dark breast band. Juveniles show some
barring below.

Numerous along northwestern coasts locally, but rare elsewhere,
it is normally seen at sea between Alaska and northern California.

Ancient and other **Murrelets** and **Auklets:** distinct (not mottled)
colors in summer and plain backs at all times. Winter **Pigeon
Guillemot:** white wing patch. Larger bird with long sleek neck.
Dovekie: tiny Atlantic sea-bird with white markings on back and
stub bill.

Black head contrasts with blue-gray back. Short pale bill, and black bib (summer adult.)

White streaks behind eye to nape give the breeding birds their "ancient" name. Dark upperparts contrast with white underparts, white underwing. The streaks and bib virtually disappear in winter, and are absent on Juveniles.

Breeding on islands in the Aleutians and Canada, it is mostly seen at sea along west coast down to California in winter. Despite stocky shape, it leaps from the water to dive after prey. Direct low-level whirring flight.

Winter **Marbled Murrelet:** prominent white back markings. **Cassin's Auklet:** smaller and grayer overall, including cheek and throat. **Xantu's, Craveri's Murrelet:** plain black above. White throat, underparts (all year,) slim bills. **Common Murre:** far larger, slender pointed bill.

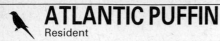

ATLANTIC PUFFIN
Resident

12in

Extraordinary triangular bill, multicolored in summer, diminishes to a less colorful smaller bill in winter.

Black crown, nape, back and wings. White underparts, off-white face and bright orange feet.

Extremely fast, whirring wing beats and splayed feet on landing typical of auks. Nests in burrows on cliff faces and tops. It winters offshore in the northern Atlantic, most commonly off Canada.

Other similar **Puffins** and **Auklets:** western, Pacific species. **Razorbills** and **Murres:** larger, with black bills, black feet. **Black Guillemot:** white wing patch, delicate pointed bill. **Dovekie:** far smaller, stub bill in all seasons.

Prominent large white wing patch, and white underwing.

Quite a delicate pointed bill. Otherwise black in summer except for red feet. Juveniles, winter adults are white with mottled brown underparts, making the wing patch indistinct. Juveniles may show brown flecks on patch. Note underwing.

Breeding across the far north and northeast on island sites in summer, it is mainly seen in whirring flight off Canada in winter. An Atlantic species, some stragglers may reach the west coast to mix with Pigeon Guillemots.

Pigeon Guillemot: white wing patch broken by dark wedge.
Common, Thick-billed Murres: very dark brown upperparts.
Razorbill: thick blunt bill, no wing patch. Winter **Puffins:** remnant of triangular summer bill still distinctive, no wing patch.
Marbled Murrelet: shorter bill, shorter neck.

111

PIGEON GUILLEMOT
Resident

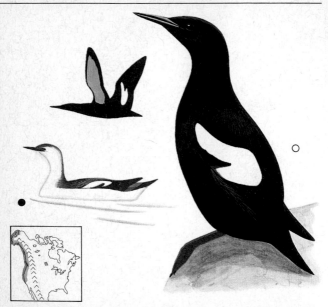

Prominent large white wing patch broken by dark wedge. Gray underwing.

Quite a delicate pointed bill. Otherwise black in summer except for red feet. Juveniles and winter adults are white with mostly dark brown upperparts, with the wedge still prominent. Note the underwing.

Breeding on Alaskan and west coast sites in summer, mainly seen offshore of the breeding areas in winter, and restricted to the north Pacific at all times. Beware confusion with the occasional Black Guillemot straggler.

Black Guillemot: white wing patch prominent and unbroken. **Common** and **Thick-billed Murres:** very dark brown upperparts, winter and summer. **Razorbill:** thick blunt-tipped bill, no white wing patch. **Marbled Murrelet:** shorter bill, shorter neck.

A large gray auklet. The heavy pale bill is adorned with a "horn" in summer. Note gray feet in flight.

Belly nearly white, underwing gray. White streaks above and behind eye, and below cheek, best seen in breeding plumage. Juveniles lack these completely. Back is darker in all ages. Note pointed wing tips.

Breeding in large colonies down burrows in summer, they can be seen in fall and winter along western coasts, sheltering in large flocks offshore. Flight is rapid but strong.

Tufted Puffin: red feet. Adults have large reddish bills, lacking on young birds. Rounded wings. **Cassin's Auklet:** far smaller, although hard to distinguish at sea, but note small dark bill with pale spot. Summer **Marbled Murrelet:** brown and mottled, much darker above. Medium pointed bill.

A large black auk with orange-red feet visible in flight. Adults have large reddish bills, lacking on young birds.

Adult is black-bodied. Head is unmistakable with white face, enlarged yellow and red bill, and yellow tassel behind the eye. Winter birds retain only the red bill. Juveniles lack even this, resembling Rhinoceros Auklet.

Abundant across the northern Pacific, they breed in coastal colonies, wintering all the way down to California. Normally seen offshore, they have a strong flight after a long run to become airborne.

Rhinoceros Auklet: confusion only possible with juvenile pattern, but note pale bill, gray feet, pointed wings. **Cassin's Auklet:** far smaller, note small dark bill with pale spot. **Atlantic Puffin:** white underparts, Atlantic range.

Whirring flight. **Large auk with dark brown upperparts, and slender pointed bill.**

Underparts white, brown-black feet. Long-necked, winter birds showing white up to chin and ear, leaving a distinct dark strip in between. Some adults are "bridled," with a line around eye and to ear. Youngsters may resemble Dovekies.

A sleek seabird. Thoroughly sea-going, flying low. Nests in cliff ledge colonies, frequently in association with other auks. It is seen widely down the west coast in winter, but restricted to Canada in the east.

Thick-billed Murre: upperparts darker. Bill heavier, especially base, with a white stripe along it. **Razorbill:** thick blunt bill with vertical stripe. **Black, Pigeon Guillemots:** smaller. Very visible white wing patch in mid-body. **Loons:** far larger. Normal wing beats. Sea-**Ducks:** "duck" bills.

Whirring flight. Thick blunt-tipped bill with a vertical stripe through it.

Upperparts and head are black, underparts white. Black feet. Immature birds have marginally slimmer bills, and white extends up to the chin and ear, but they still strongly resemble adults.

A thick-set auk with typical sea-going habits, nesting in cliff-ledge colonies, frequently in association with murres and guillemots. Flight over the sea is low on rapid wingbeats. This is a species of the northern Atlantic.

Murres and **Guillemots:** similar size, although sleeker, and appear black and white at a distance. Bills are much more slender and pointed.

THICK-BILLED MURRE

18in

Resident

Whirring flight. Large auk with blackish brown upperparts, and pointed bill (rather thick at base) with a white stripe along the upper mandible.

Underparts are white, rising to a point beneath the chin. Feet are brown. Winter birds develop white on throat to chin only, unlike Common Murre, a useful distinguishing feature in winter months.

A sleek seabird. Thoroughly sea-going with low flight. Nests in cliff ledge colonies, frequently in association with other auks. Range extends further down east coast, less down west than that of Common Murre.

Common Murre: dark brown upperparts. Bill is slender, pointed. **Razorbill:** thick blunt-tipped bill with a vertical stripe. **Black** and **Pigeon Guillemots:** smaller with very visible white wing patches in mid-bodies. **Loons:** far larger with normal wing beats. Sea-**Ducks:** "duck" bills.

117

Snowy Egret (1) 24in Res/ Summer Vis. Black bill & legs, bright yellow feet. Plumes when breeding. Frantic feeding action: disturbs prey with feet & stabs at it. Common in mangroves, swamps, ponds.

White Ibis (2) 25in Res/Summer Vis. Long downcurved bill. White underparts at all ages, adults almost all white. Red bill, legs, face in adults. Common locally in mangrove swamps & marshes.

Tricolored Heron (3) 26in Res/ Summer Vis. Long, white foreneck, mainly gray-blue upperparts. White belly. Not common. Usually in southeast mangrove swamps and salt marshes on coast.

Great Egret (4) 39in Res/Int. Mig. Yellow dagger-like bill, long black legs & feet. Plumes when breeding. Stealthy hunter. Common in mangrove swamps, marshes, mud flats.

Sharp-tailed Sparrow (1) 5½in
Int. Mig. Gray crown stripe, gray
triangle on ear coverts
surrounnded by orange/buff.
Spiked tail feathers. Common,
can be hard to find in grasses.
Widespread in summer.

Seaside Sparrow (2) 6in Res.
Yellow patch between eye & bill.
White chin. Spiked tail feathers.
Various forms according to
range, some now rare. Coastal
tidal marshes.

Little Blue Heron (3) 24in Res/
Summer Vis. Gray bill tipped
black. Adult: whole body slate-
blue, purple neck. Immature: all
white. Deliberate stalking
technique. Common on coastal
wetlands, ponds.

Snow Goose (4) 30in Winter
Vis./Int. Mig. Pied with
"grinning" pink bill. "Blue"
phase: dark body & wings.
"White" phase: only wing tips
dark. Breeds in Arctic. Common
winter visitor to Gulf Coast.

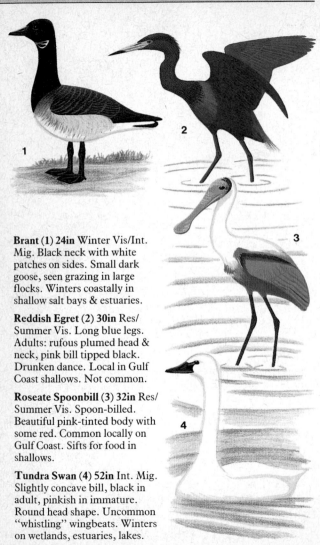

Brant (1) 24in Winter Vis/Int. Mig. Black neck with white patches on sides. Small dark goose, seen grazing in large flocks. Winters coastally in shallow salt bays & estuaries.

Reddish Egret (2) 30in Res/ Summer Vis. Long blue legs. Adults: rufous plumed head & neck, pink bill tipped black. Drunken dance. Local in Gulf Coast shallows. Not common.

Roseate Spoonbill (3) 32in Res/ Summer Vis. Spoon-billed. Beautiful pink-tinted body with some red. Common locally on Gulf Coast. Sifts for food in shallows.

Tundra Swan (4) 52in Int. Mig. Slightly concave bill, black in adult, pinkish in immature. Round head shape. Uncommon "whistling" wingbeats. Winters on wetlands, estuaries, lakes.

Water Pipit (1) 6½in Int. Mig.
Thin bill, plain gray-brown back,
white outer tail feathers. Bobs tail
repeatedly. Streaked buff
underparts. Walks rather than
hops. Winters across south,
particularly on beaches.

Horned Lark (2) 7½in Res/Int.
Mig. Black "horns" & cheek
pattern. Black upper breast band,
dark undertail. Walks rather than
hops. Numerous. Beaches &
inland.

Peregrine Falcon (3) 15–19in
Int. Migrant. Clear dark/black
crown, nape & heavy mustache.
Preys on other birds, swooping at
high speed for a kill. Migrates to
east coast in winter, seen around
cliffs.

Bald Eagle (4) 30–42in Res/Int.
Mig. Mig. Huge size & white
head in adults. Immatures: white
areas on inner underwing.
National bird of USA, now
recovering its numbers. Fishes
along coasts & rivers.

Index and check-list

Keep a record of your sightings by checking the box.